Star Quilts

The Classic QUILT Series #7

LAURA NOWNES

The Quilt Digest Press

Project direction by Michael Kile.
Editorial direction by Harold Nadel.
Book and cover design by Kajun Graphics.
Quilt, cover and room setting photographs by
Sharon Risedorph.
Computer graphics by Kandy Petersen.
Typographical composition by DC Typography.
Printed by Nissha Printing Company, Ltd., Kyoto, Japan.
Color separations by the printer.
Homes graciously lent by Linda Reuther and Margaret
Peters.
The author extends special thanks to Alex Anderson,
Michael Kile and Bill Folk. Thanks also to Glendora
Hutson for her generous sharing of her technique for
constructing *LeMoyne Star.*

For my little Molly Bear, with love.

First Printing.

Library of Congress Cataloging-in-Publication Data

Nownes, Laura, 1953-
    Star quilts / Laura Nownes.
        p.   cm. – (The classic quilt series : #7)
    ISBN 0-913327-26-3 (ppr) : $6.95
    1. Patchwork–Patterns. 2. Quilting–Patterns. I. Title.
    II. Series : Nownes, Laura, 1953- Classic quilt series : #7.
    TT835.N72   1991
    746.9′7– dc20   90-28955
                                                                    CIP

The Quilt Digest Press
P.O. Box 1331
Gualala, CA 95445

INTRODUCTION

As you have already noticed, the quilts in this book are incredibly beautiful and different from the majority of *Star* quilts you've seen before, even though we use classic patterns.

I chose to work on this project with Alex Anderson, a talented designer, quiltmaker and instructor in the San Francisco area. With her individualistic style and creative imagination, Alex has taken the familiar patterns and breathed new life into them: they sparkle with energy. She has taken a fresh look at the traditional blocks, working with them to create *Star* quilts that reflect her energetic personality. The resulting blends of color and fabric are magic to the eye.

For the first three quilts in the book, we worked within the traditional guidelines and settings, but the fabric choices may surprise you. For the fourth quilt, Alex combined the three traditional blocks in an original setting, creating an unusually striking quilt.

With the help of this book, you will never see *Star* quilts in the same old way; you will be inspired to challenge youself, to dare to use different colors and fabrics, to create your own vibrant, sparkling quilts.

Happy quilting!

Laura

Laura Nownes

WHAT YOU NEED

Fabric: 100% cotton; see individual quilts for exact
    amounts
Glass-head pins
C-Thru plastic ruler
Sewing machine or hand sewing needle
100% cotton thread
Steam iron
Light-colored towel
Pressing surface
For traditional cutting:
    Template plastic
    Ultra-fine permanent pen
    Paper scissors
    Fabric scissors
    Marking pencil
For quick cutting:
    Rotary cutter
    Cutting board
    Wide plastic ruler

GENERAL INSTRUCTIONS

Complete yardage charts and assembly instructions
are given for making each of the four *Star* quilts in
this book. Accurate template patterns are found in the
back of the book if you wish to use traditional
methods of cutting and piecing. However, quick-
cutting and sewing can be used if you so desire. There
are so many useful tools and techniques available to
the quiltmaker today to help make the job easier and
save time. Here are a few suggestions to guide you
with quick-cutting and sewing methods.

*Remember, accuracy in cutting and sewing is
important to the success of your quilt.*

Quick-Cutting Tips

Always measure the template pattern first to deter-
mine the
    • To cut squares: simply cut strips the required
width and then cut each strip into squares, as shown.

• To cut triangles with the grainline running as
shown: simply cut squares the size of one of the
shorter sides and then cut them in half diagonally,
as shown.

• To cut triangles with the grainline running as
shown: simply cut squares the size of the longest side
and then cut the square into quarters diagonally,
as shown.

• To cut triangles similar to the one shown: simply
cut a strip of fabric the width indicated by the arrow.
Then use your template to mark and cut the
triangles, as shown.

 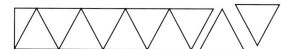

• To cut triangles similar to the one shown: simply
use the measurement of the template pattern to cut
rectangles, as shown. Then cut the rectangles in
half diagonally, as shown.

• To cut diamonds: simply cut strips using the measurement from your template pattern as indicated
in the illustration. Then use your template pattern to
mark and cut the diamonds, as shown.

Sewing Tips

• Use a ¼″ seam allowance throughout.

• Press often, pressing the seams toward the darker fabric whenever possible, except in the case of the *LeMoyne Star*. For this pattern you must press the seams joining diamonds open, in order to achieve a flat star center.

• Whenever possible, run several pairs of fabric shapes through your machine without breaking the chain of thread joining them, to save time.

• When joining a bias edge to a straight-grain edge, sew with the straight-grain-edged shape on top to avoid stretching.

• To prevent cutting off star points, stitch with the point on top in order to see that the stitching line does not extend beyond the point, as shown.

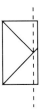

• Take time to measure your joined blocks and to cut and mark the borders accurately before joining them, to avoid rippled edges.

VARIABLE STAR

Pieced by Alex Anderson and hand quilted by Mary Hershberger.

6″ Block	CRIB/WALL	TWIN	DOUBLE/QUEEN	KING
Finished size	42″ × 51″	68″ × 85″	85″ × 85″	93″ × 93″
Blocks set	4 × 5	7 × 9	9 × 9	10 × 10
Total star blocks	20	63	81	100
Total alternate blocks	12	48	64	81
Total side triangles	14	28	32	36

FABRIC NEEDED (YARDS)

Light Background for star blocks	1	2	2½	3
Fabric for stars	1	2¼	2¾	3¼
Alternate blocks, side and corner triangles, and light of sawtooth border	1½	3	3¾	4⅝
Inside border: two fabrics to total (cut crossgrain)	⅜	½	½	¾
Sawtooth border: two dark fabrics to total	½	¾	1	1
Backing	1⅝	5	7½	8¼
Binding	½	¾	⅞	1

CUTTING YOUR FABRIC

Use templates A, F and H.

Light background:				
Template A, number of 2½″ squares	80	252	324	400
Template F	80	252	324	400
Stars:				
Template A	20	63	81	100
Template F	240	756	972	1200
Alternate blocks: number of 6½″ squares	12	48	64	81
Side triangles: number of 9¾″ squares cut into quarters diagonally	4	7	8	9
Corner triangles: number of 5″ squares cut in half diagonally	2	2	2	2
Inner border: width	1½″	1½″	1½″	1½″
Sawtooth border: Template H, light and dark, *each*	52	60	84	104
Backing: number of lengths	1	2	3	3

PUTTING IT ALL TOGETHER

1. Make the required number of pieced blocks, as shown.
2. Lay out all of the pieced blocks, alternate blocks, side and corner triangles in a desired color arrangement.
3. Join the pieced blocks to the alternate blocks and side and corner triangles in a diagonal setting.
4. Attach the inner borders. The borders on the sample quilt were pieced. Crossgrain-cut strips of fabric were joined to achieve the required length for each side.
5. Construct half-square triangles, as shown. Then join to make sawtooth borders.
6. Layer your backing, batting and quilt top in preparation for quilting.

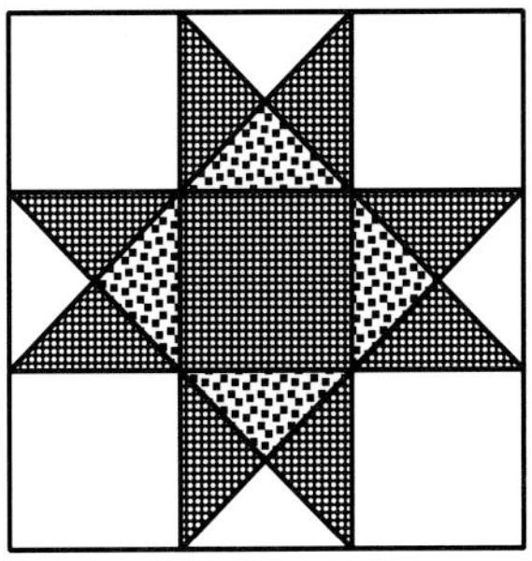

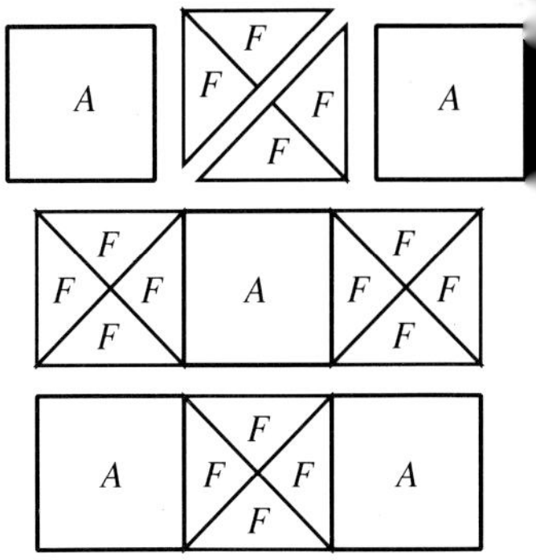

Step 1

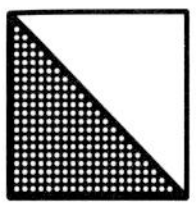

Step 5

Pieced by Alex Anderson and hand quilted by Mary Hershberger.

10½″ Block	WALL	TWIN	DOUBLE/QUEEN	KING
Finished size	66″×66″	77″×88″	88″×88″	98″×98″
Blocks set	5×5	6×7	7×7	8×8
Total blocks	25	42	49	64

FABRIC NEEDED (YARDS)

	WALL	TWIN	DOUBLE/QUEEN	KING
Background: three fabrics to total	2	3	3½	4½
Stars: total amount (extra allowed for pieced diamonds)	2	3	3½	4½
Inside border (cut crossgrain)	⅜	⅜	⅝	⅝
Outside border	2	2½	2½	2⅞
Backing	4	5¼	8	8½
Binding	⅝	¾	1	1

CUTTING YOUR FABRIC

Use templates C, D, G, O and M.

	WALL	TWIN	DOUBLE/QUEEN	KING
Background:				
Template C, number of 3⅝″ squares	100	168	196	256
Template D	100	168	196	256
Stars: Template G*	200	336	392	512
Inside border: width (cut crossgrain)	2″	2″	2″	2″
Outside border: width (cut lengthwise)	6″	6″	6″	6″
Backing: number of lengths	2	2	3	3

*For split diamonds substitute **Template O** (two for each diamond) and for stripped diamonds substitute **Template M** (three for each diamond).

PUTTING IT ALL TOGETHER

The pictured quilt has the traditional *LeMoyne Star* as well as two pieced variations. Illustrations are given for constructing each type. *You can make as many of each as you choose.*

1. Make the required number of pieced blocks, as shown. To achieve a flat star center you must not allow your stitches to extend into the seam allowance. Begin and end your stitches at the dots, as shown.

2. Lay your pieced blocks out in a desired color arrangement. Then join them together in a straight setting.

3. Attach the inner borders. The sample quilt used strips of fabric cut crossgrain.

4. Attach the outer borders.

5. Layer your backing, batting and quilt top in preparation for quilting.

Pieced variations:

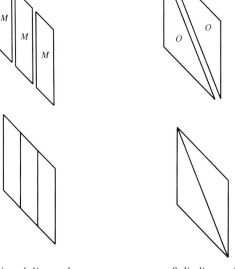

Stripped diamonds   Split diamonds

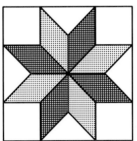

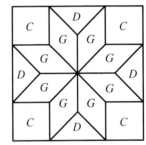

For each star make four:

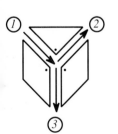

Press open

Make four:

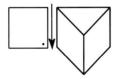

Make two:

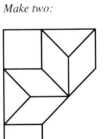

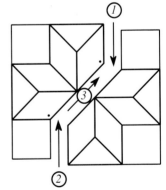

①& ② Press seam toward star

③ Press seam open

Step 1

Pieced and appliquéd by Alex Anderson and hand quilted by Kristina Volker.

12″ Block	WALL	TWIN	DOUBLE/QUEEN	KING
Finished size	71″ × 71″	71″ × 95″	95″ × 95″	107″ × 107″
Blocks set	5 × 5	5 × 7	7 × 7	8 × 8
Total blocks	25	35	49	64

FABRIC NEEDED (YARDS)

	WALL	TWIN	DOUBLE/QUEEN	KING
Light background	2½	2¾	3¾	5¼
Stars: fabric to total	2¾	3¾	5¼	6¾
Inside border	1¾	2½	2½	2⅞
Outside border	2¼	2⅞	2⅞	3¼
Backing	4½	5¾	8½	9½
Binding	¾	¾	1	1

CUTTING YOUR FABRIC

Use templates B, E, I, L, N and P.

	WALL	TWIN	DOUBLE/QUEEN	KING
Light background:				
Template I	200	280	392	512
Template E	100	140	196	256
Template P	100	140	196	256
Stars:				
Template B	25	35	49	64
Template I	200	280	392	512
Template N	100 & 100R*	140 & 140R*	196 & 196R*	256 & 256R*
Template L	100	140	196	256
Inside border: width	1″	1″	1″	1″
Outside border: width	5½″	5½″	5½″	5½″
Backing: number of lengths	2	2	3	3

*R = reverse template on fabric

PUTTING IT ALL TOGETHER

1. Make the required number of pieced blocks, as shown.

2. Lay your pieced blocks out in a desired color arrangement. Then join them together in a straight setting.

3. Attach the inner and outer borders.

4. Layer your backing, batting and quilt top in preparation for quilting.

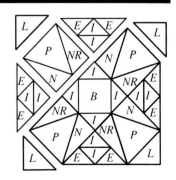

Step 1

Pieced by Alex Anderson and machine quilted by Margaret Gair.

*6" **Variable Star***
*10½" **LeMoyne Star***
*12" **1904 Star***

Finished size   *72" × 72"*

FABRIC NEEDED (YARDS)

For quilt top: scraps to total	9
Backing	5
Binding	¾

CUTTING YOUR FABRIC

Use templates A, B, C, D, E, F, G, I, J, K, L, M, N, O, P and Q.

For *1904 Star* (Make 4):

Template B	4
Template I	48
Template E	32
Template N	16 & 16R*
Template P	16
Template L	16

*R = reverse template on fabric

For inner *Flying Geese* border (Make 72 units):

Template J (light)	144
Template Q (dark)	72

For *Variable Star* (Make 24):

Template A	120
Template F	384

For *LeMoyne Star* (Make 20):

Template C	80
Template D	80
Template G*	160

*For split diamonds substitute **Template O** (two for each diamond) and for stripped diamonds substitute **Template M** (three for each diamond).

For outer *Flying Geese* border
(Make 120 units):

Template K (dark)	240
Template D (light)	120
Backing: number of lengths	2

1. Make four *1904 Star* blocks, as shown.

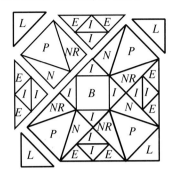

2. Make 72 *Flying Geese* units for the inner border, as shown.

From these units, make: four sets of 16 each

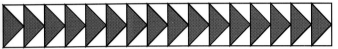

and four corner units

3. Make twenty-four *Variable Star* blocks, as shown.

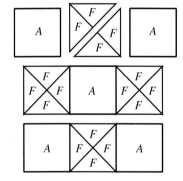

4. Make twenty *LeMoyne Star* blocks, as shown. Note that some can have split diamonds and some can have stripped diamonds.

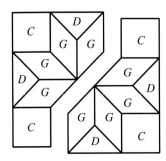

5. Make 120 *Flying Geese* units for the outer border, as shown.

From these units, make:

four corner units   four sets of 28 each

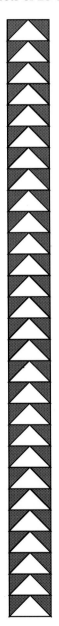

6. Lay out all of the blocks and borders, referring to the photo for the exact placement, or using your own placement.

7. Join the blocks and borders together to complete the quilt top.

8. Layer the backing, batting and quilt top in preparation for quilting.

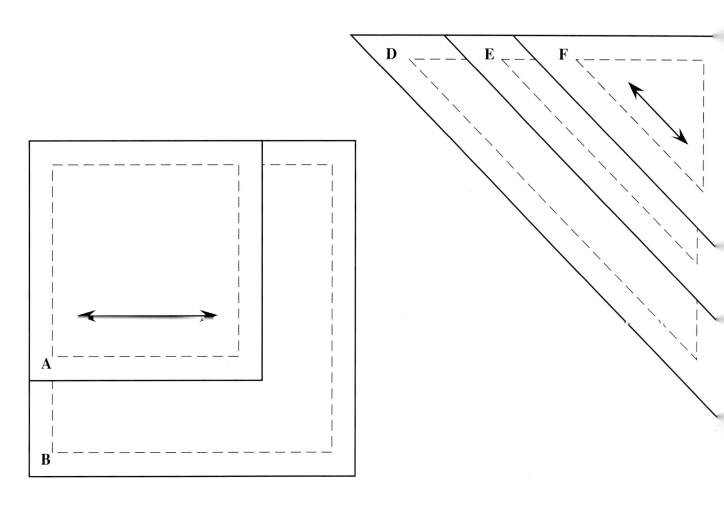

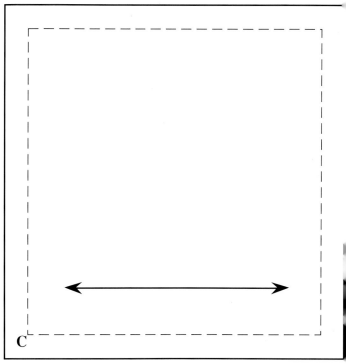

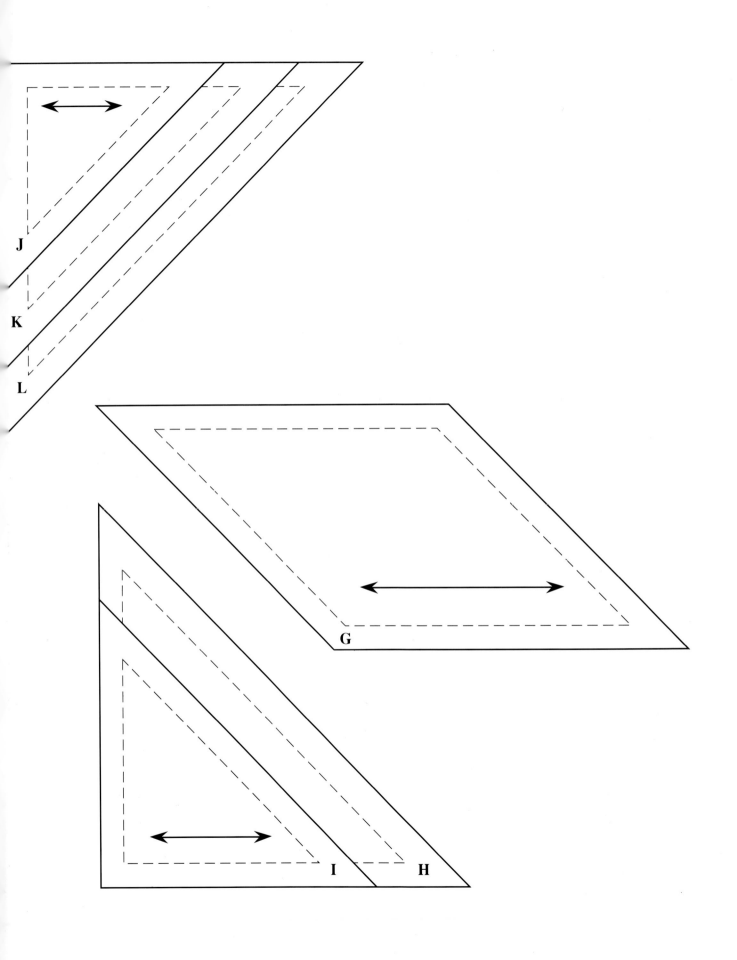

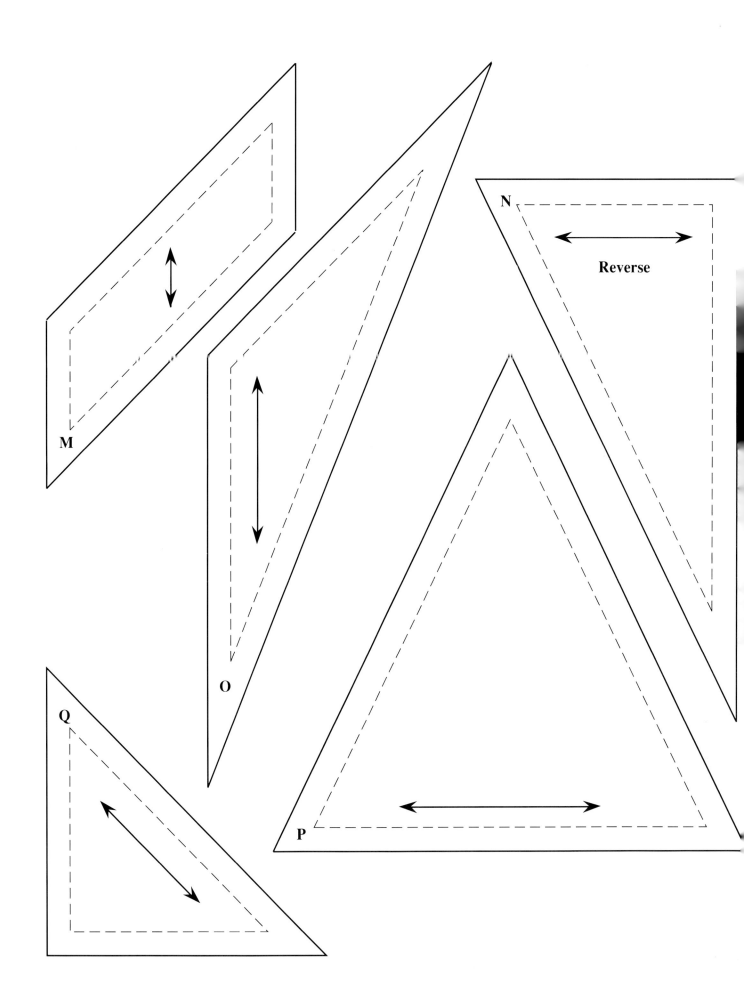

M

N

Reverse

O

P

Q

Simply the Best

*W*hen we started our publishing efforts in 1983, we made one pledge to ourselves: to produce the finest quilt books imaginable. The critics and our loyal readers clearly believe that we're living up to that promise.

In a time when thin, 64-page quilt books with only staples to hold their pages intact and small numbers of color photos sell for as much as $19.95, we are proud that our books set a noticeably higher standard.

Books from The Quilt Digest Press are hefty, with many more pages and masses of color photos. They are printed on high-quality satin-finish paper and are bound with durable glues and spines to last a lifetime. The world's finest quilt photographer does all our work. A great design team lavishes its attention on every detail of every page. And the world's finest commercial printer sees to it that every book is a gem. Add knowledgeable authors with vital ideas and you, too, will say, "The Quilt Digest Press? Oh, they're Simply the Best."

Try another of our books. They're as good as the one in your hands. And write for our free color catalogue.

THE QUILT DIGEST PRESS

Dept. D
P.O. Box 1331
Gualala, CA 95445